MW00718382

SUMMER JOB SUCCESS
(AND BEYOND)

By Edward DeJesus
Revised Edition, First printing
Copyright 2019 by Edward DeJesus

1st Edition, 1st printing

DeJesus Solutions, LLC
www.edwarddejesus.com

ISBN: 978-0-578-48141-8

Library of Congress Control Number:
2019903546

DEDICATION

To the youth who are seeking opportunities, the people who are willing to provide them, and my family for supporting me in being the latter.

TABLE OF CONTENTS

"Successful young people don't chase jobs; jobs chase them."
-Edward DeJesus

Introduction: Welcome to the Summer

Trey wiped his forehead with the back of his arm and glanced out over the neighboring houses before turning to his teammates beside him on the roof where they had just finished installing their first real solar panels. His arms had only stopped aching from so much unfamiliar work last week, and this new-found strength excited him. Working with his body had been more taxing than he'd anticipated – and that wasn't even considering the whole morning-routine-thing. But after some adjusting, Trey had started to enjoy that quiet morning cup of coffee, carpooling with his new coworkers and making small talk over the truck's gentle rattle. But even that didn't make every day easy, just that morning, he'd ignored another text from his friend Luke – the third of its kind in about two weeks: *"Yo man, call in sick. We're going pool hopping and I got the booze and weed."*

He could see Luke and their crew now, living it up, quarters scrounged together to score enough booze to carry them through the night. They were probably already lounging in front of some pool at an apartment complex. When Trey signed up for the "Green Economy" summer job program, his friends had given him a little grief: missing their summer plans? For work? Trey had never shown the slightest motivation to earn money, as far as they were concerned, let alone care about the environment.

But the truth was that Trey had thought about it many times before. His crew just wasn't the types that you talked about something like that with. So he usually just brushed his thoughts of work aside, content to smoke and drink with his friends, until one day when an older man with a stooped posture and wrinkles that made him look fifteen years older than he was bought Trey and his friends some booze. That man had looked at him with unfocused eyes and said, "I was like y'all at your age, too," and laughed, as if they were in on the same secret. Trey then watched him shuffle away and get into an old hooptie with a rusted-out bottom, clanking out of the parking lot. Trey's stomach had dropped. Did he want to be hanging around liquor stores in a decrepit car, wrinkled before his time?

Trey shook the cobwebs of the memory of the man from his head, silently thanking him for that look. Trey jumped back on the impact drill to make holes in the rafters like he'd been taught. The noise cleared his head. Stretching his back under the afternoon sun, he turned to help his work crew pack up. As they drove back, Trey finally shot Luke a text: *sorry man, gotta do what I gotta do.*

As he climbed into bed that night, Trey was uneasy. He had been doing alright in the summer job so far, but it ended in three weeks. Three weeks from now, he'd be right back there, with Luke and everyone else, getting high. That thought followed him into his dreams, which were thick with anxious loops of him staring in the mirror, his face lined in deep wrinkles and all of his teeth falling out. The next morning, he pulled on each tooth before brushing to make sure they were still solid and there. As he got dressed, he shook his head and resolved to make the most of his last three weeks. There was no way he'd return to square one. No way.

When he got into work, Trey decided to push himself for the first time, taking initiative on the job. He volunteered to do more of the tasks, and went out of his way to offer help to coworkers if they seemed behind. Each time he finished his own task, he hopped over to his boss, Tina, and asked her how else he could help.

It wasn't until the third day of this newfound dedication that Tina noticed his drive. She turned and looked at him squinting her eyes and smiling. "You're a real go-getter, huh?"

He grinned. "Yes, ma'am. I guess I am."

She nodded, half to him, half to herself. "That's good."

The next three weeks passed swiftly, with Trey working extra, taking on tasks, and getting some off-the-cuff experience with the computer systems that were used to lay out the solar array. He spoke frequently with all the full-time workers and made sure he knew their favorite lunch drink. Every morning Trey would stop at the local corner store to buy an assortment of his coworker's favorite beverages, from Diet Cokes to Kombucha. At lunch, he handed out each drink personally taking advantage of the few minutes to check in with his colleagues and his day's performance. Everybody loved Trey. Trey was the man.

Tina had been working in the industry for over a decade. She'd shown Trey the how-to and taken an interest in his improvement. After handing her her favorite afternoon beverage, Trey asked her how she managed to land her first job in the industry. To his surprise Tina stated that she started out just like him, just not as well liked. She offered to put in a good word for him if he wanted to continue working with the company after school hours. Trey couldn't believe Tina's willingness to help.

Immediately, he emailed her the resume that he completed with the help of the program staff. The last few days, Trey was a bundle of nerves, not knowing if Tina had sent his resume over to the main office. He filled out a few applications at local fast food joints even though it wasn't part of his plan.

On the last day of summer, Tina ordered in some pizza to celebrate Trey's last day. During the lunch, Tina introduced Trey to Mr. Dotson, the regional area vice-president and in charge of hiring. Mr. Dotson told Trey that he heard wonderful things about his performance and wanted to know if he would be interested in working part-time, after school.

In the parking lot, after the day was done, Trey sighed, he checked his teeth in his phone, and walked over to Tina to thank her, "Because of you, I got a dream job and can really get my life on track. Thank you."

Tina smiled. "That was all you."

Trey's dedication to making the most of his summer job program changed his life – and you can do the same. If you're reading this, chances are you're taking part or interested in a summer job program. That plunge is a meaningful pivot to making the most of the rest of your life – congratulations! Through your summer job program, you'll find the drive inside of you and put it towards creating the kind of life you want.

Each year, hundreds of thousands of young people nationwide join the workforce, either by finding jobs in their neighborhood or by attending summer job programs like yourself. These summer job programs do more than just land you experience: according to research from 2018, young people who take part in summer job programs are significantly less likely to get caught up in the criminal justice system. And more than that, for young people of color on the older end of the spectrum, their employment grew by 7% and wages jumped up 12%[1]. A lot of this data points to these programs being so important that they actually serve as a pivotal springboard for closing the gap in racial inequalities in the workforce. How's that for power?

But a summer job program isn't some magic blank check that solves all your problems: you have to put hard work into it to build the kind of future you want. The best way to do that? Reflect on what kind of life you want one year from your program's start date.

Close your eyes and visualize your ideal life a year from now. How will you be doing in school? Where will you be living? What type of part-time job do you want? How do you want to feel financially? The more details, the better. Picture what you're holding in your hand, the kinds of clothes you're wearing, the people you'll be with. Use all five senses. Do you have an image in your head? Good. Now spend about ten minutes writing your reflections down, either in the space below or in your own journal if you have one. Considering this level of detail may seem silly, but it's actually extremely helpful in guiding you to positioning yourself for success in the long-term by looking beyond your own present moment. The more details you have in hand, the more achievable the ideal will feel right now.

My Life in One Year

Once you've written it all down, you should have a good foundation outlining what you're looking for - and what you're not. With these visions in hand, you're ready to get going on building your future now. Why wait?

Having an end goal helps you backtrack to figure out how to get to each stepping stone along the way. But remember, no person is an island, and asking others who came before you how to make the most of your program is a powerful way to get advice you might otherwise have never found out. We call this our Universal Success Law: young people who learn on trial and error will always lose to young people who learn on others' trial and error. Think about it. Why make mistakes that have been made hundreds of times before, when you can learn from the folks who already made those mistakes. Each mistake that could have been avoided puts you that much further behind the other young people who learned how to avoid those pitfalls from the get-go.

You can find successful people to talk to everywhere. Find a summer program graduate who's gotten a job - ask around, email summer pro-gram advisors, or look to members of your community - and write their name, contact information, and a plan for when to contact them in the box below.

Let's get to work!	
Summer Program Graduate:	
Contact Info:	
When will you talk to them?	

Once you have the plan set for contacting them, don't put it off. Give the person a call as soon as you can (meeting them in person is best) and ask them the following questions, putting their answers in the spaces below:

What did they do to get the most out of the program?	
What did they do to bring their success in the program into the real world?	
What was the most challenging part of the program and how did they handle it?	
What advice do they have about being the best success they can?	

With all of this information in your pocket, what is one thing you can do on the first day of your summer job program to make the most of it?

_____

_____

_____

By opening this book and taking the first steps to a summer job or summer job program, you've demonstrated that you have it in you to follow your path to abundant future economic opportunities (FEOs). Congratulations—you've made it to the starting line.

Ch 1: How Summer Job Programs Got their Start

Minors have always worked. Thousands of years ago, children were instrumental to farming and nomadic cultures, working fields, tending livestock, or helping take care of babies. As societies shifted from mostly agrarian to an industrialized economy, public education became the norm, preparing young people to take their places as factory workers, shop managers, and bookkeepers of tomorrow. Factory owners needed a workforce who would show up on time and do what they were told. The traditional school systems were ideal for teaching this to children. However, youth labor was exploited and young people found themselves in the deadliest jobs because they weren't taught to share their opinion or push for better. Thankfully, national labor laws were put in place to protect the growth and wellbeing of children, not the factories.

Nowadays, the majority of young people can't work at conventional jobs until they're sixteen – and even then, there are many protections and limitations in place to keep them from being taken advantage of and to make sure they focus in school. But even today, many young people find themselves stuck in work without protections nationwide. And all too often, with schooling resources distributed so unevenly, the picture painted looks much like it did before: the wealthy bursting with opportunities to grow their economic situation, while the majority scramble for a route up and out.

With the help of summer job programs, many cities and counties are hard at work changing that reality. Job programs are part of our country's more recent history, dating back to the 1960s when then-President Lyndon B. Johnson initiated the first nationwide program with the hope of fighting poverty. Since then, programs have evolved well past Johnson's first vision to include hundreds of statewide, local, private, and nonprofit job opportunity programs with structures as varied as the far-reaching, option rich Job Corps, to more targeted programs such as GRID Alternatives, the California-based program training young people to work within the solar industry. Programs have also grown to be more focused on catering to individual needs, and programs abound for underserved population, justice-involved, youth with disabilities, and those with other specific needs. Each program offers something slightly different, but they all have one major thing in common: a dedication to your best interest.

Before you go diving into the first summer job program that stumbles across your path, make sure you've looked through all your options, so you know you're choosing the one that's the absolute best for you. These days, summer job programs take many shapes and follow different norms, goals, and visions for success:

Subsidized programs are ones where your wages and some of the costs for your employment are offset by a third party, usually a government agency or a non-profit organization. Subsidized summer programs are designed to ensure that underserved youth and young adults get an opportunity to develop much needed work experience. The majority of subsidized summer job placements are in the public sector (federal, state, city and non-profit institutions). One of the best perks of subsidized summer employment opportunities are how locally connected and community-oriented they are – a huge bonus when you find yourself at the end of the program and in need of additional opportunities. The connections you can make in locally-funded programs may help you land additional training, certifications and access to important resources. You can find programs geared toward girls and young women, communities of color, people with disabilities, previously-incarcerated youth, and more. If you so choose, you have the opportunity to take part in programs well-versed in your community's needs and chal-lenges in the workforce that other communities may not have to contend with.

Unsubsidized programs are ones where all costs of your employment are borne by the employer. However, through innovative partnerships the employer will assume the costs of employment while many school and workforce agencies assume the responsibilities of job coaching, providing support services and basically doing whatever needs to be done to ensure that you have a positive learning experience and contribute productively to the goals of the company. Unsubsidized programs are harder to come by and usually go to the most job-ready student who has the most social capital.

No matter if you're looking to get into a trade that will one day land you an office on the top floor of a skyscraper, or you'd be rather be working on getting those skyscrapers built in the first place, there's a summer job program that can help your dreams get going.

Whatever avenue you choose to take, know that you have options out there – probably more than you thought. Download a copy of the DeJesus Solutions National Summer Job Directory at www.edwarddejesus.com and contact a local workforce agency near you. Each board has experts on staff that can guide you and your family though the range of summer and year-round work experience opportunities available in your city.

Here are some questions you should ask when you contact the agencies:

1.   What summer job opportunities are available for a young person aged __?

2.   What are the requirements for entry?

3.   Are any of these programs tied to an industry certified credential?

4.   What is the first step that I should take if I am interested in one of these opportunities?

Write down the programs you learn about in the chart below:

Let's get to work!		
Type of Program	Program Title	Contact Info and Address

Which one best aligns with that ideal future you wrote down earlier?

_____

_____

Which program can you get to reliably each day?

_____

_____

Which program seems like they'd get you the most?

_____

_____

Maybe most importantly, which program's schedule (including start dates, end dates, and cut-off dates for applying) fit in with your own schedule?

Circle the program that ticks off the most boxes for the questions above. Then, choose a friend who's willing to go down to the program's office to scope it out in person with you – maybe that friend could be someone looking for a summer job themselves. Going down to meet the people in charge face-to-face is the best way to figure out if the program feels like the right fit for you, and program coordinators will appreciate such a personable move.

Which program will you visit first?	
Who's going with you to check it out?	
When will you go?	

When you visit, take notes here to keep track of what you've learned about the program and how to get the ball rolling. Here are some questions you should ask during your visit:

How does the program define success and what is the success rate?

What are three things that most young people like about the programs?

What are three things that they don't like?

What opportunities are there to gain industry recognized credentials?

How many work experience sites do you have and how do you determine who is selected for those sites?

What is the pay schedule and how much are we paid?

Are there any scholarship opportunities or future educational assistance opportunities available?

_____

_____

_____

_____

_____

_____

_____

_____

_____

_____

_____

If the place you and your friend scoped out doesn't feel like the right fit, don't be discouraged. Select the next program you were considering and try again, visiting in person to get more information. Keep going until you find the best place for your needs. Each time you hunt down information, remember that this part of the journey is never time you wasted, even if you keep not finding "the one." As long as you're learning more about what does and doesn't work for you, you're emerging from each day equipped with more knowledge than before.

As you go, you're going to discover more about what you're looking for - and your idea of the future one year from now may evolve. That's okay. Go back and write notes in the margins of the last chapter's visualization when you think of something else you'd like to have in that ideal future. Using a different ink is best so you can see how you've grown and the evolution of your vision. You've got a journey cut out for you, but all these processes together are helping you whittle down your options to leave behind a clear place for you to start out growing your FEO. Just start the process early. Summer job slots fill up fast. We recommended starting your investigation in early January.

Ch 2: What's the Point of a Summer Job?

If you're reading this, you're probably interested in landing a summer job. But do you know why you want one? Don't think about it too hard – jot down the number one reason that comes to mind for landing a summer job:

There are a million different ways to answer that, and all of them are valid. Most often, however, young people looking for a job have one thing in mind: getting that paper. But have you stopped to consider just how beneficial a summer job really is? What's the point, besides just the extra income? Landing a summer job gets you five key things that give you a leg up in any endeavors down the line:

1.   Skills

It almost goes without saying that any job you put yourself to will give you a skill that can help you down the line. One skill that all jobs teach you is time management. When you're in high school, each hour is carved out and dictated by someone else. Your parents may even still be waking you up. But when you move out of the house, whether that's for college or a job, you'll be in for a rude awakening once nobody's there to help you get your chores done. With any job, you learn valuable time-management skills that ripple out beyond the work-place. When you know how to balance your time, take care of your tasks, and hold yourself accountable, every other aspect of adulting locks into place that much more easily.

2. Credentials

Jobs, when approached with intention and motivation, pave the way for our best credentials. Some summer job programs give you the opportunity to show your proficiency or understanding of a certain aspect of your tasks. And in any job, you're meeting new people and getting the opportunity to learn about what kinds of credentials they have and recommend to thrive in the work-place. Ask the people you work with where they got their credentials and what they liked (or disliked) about their program. When you know next steps, or at least have ideas of the kinds of credentials you need to lock in success, you'll find other aspects of your life feel easier as you move through your life with confidence. At its most basic, having a job proves to yourself that you are reliable and capable, and shows how easily you can adapt to new or difficult situations. Earning money for yourself feels good and empowers you to dream of something bigger – and start looking at what credentials you need to earn to get there. Who would you be if you weren't afraid?

3. Work Experience

There isn't much that's worse for job-hunting than a blank resume and no references. Having a summer job saves you from the headache of trying to land jobs down the road without any experience under your belt. If you struggle to score that first paid opportunity, consider volunteering – it's a powerful way to make connections and fill that resume, so that next time, you're getting paid. Simply having work experience for your resume shows that you can show up when needed and be punctual, at a bare minimum.

Getting work experience is about so much more than just filling up your resume. It's about identifying what you want to do or what skills you want to develop. It goes beyond just reading over the skills you need in order to be a social media manager: can you be on a computer all day? Make cold calls to strangers? Read extensively on the latest trends and analyze data? Working a beginner's job, like at a call center or as a brand ambassador, can help you determine whether that is something that you're truly compelled to do. Take Linda, for example. She hadn't been doing well in school, but always figured she'd work with kids in a daycare - crafting, dress up, and naptime sounded easy enough, right? Linda waited until barely graduating high school before applying for jobs working with kids. Once she got hired and started the job that was supposed to be her dream, she realized she hated working with kids - they sneezed all the time, were rude, and got paint on her clothes. But because Linda hadn't explored her options earlier, she felt trapped in the childcare industry, unsure of what else she'd like to do.

What if Linda had gone ahead and worked at a day summer camp the summer between her junior and senior year? If she'd done that, she may have realized then that kids weren't her cup of tea. Instead, although Linda was frustrated to realize that her daydream hadn't been as fun as she'd hoped, she would have had her last year of high school to consider her options. While she'd been working at the summer camp, maybe the only thing she'd really enjoyed was the fabric arts classes. With that knowledge, she could have looked at programs and enrolled in courses in this area. Eventually, she could have worked her way through community college classes and certifications to study costume design in college - and now work in Hollywood. All because she'd decided to try out a summer job and identify her strengths.

4.   Education
Which version of Linda would you rather be? If you put the energy into landing a summer job that works for you, you'll narrow down what types of educational opportunities to seek

that line up with what the job has told you about yourself and your own goals. Like with credentials, working with older adults lets you in on what kinds of education you need to seek to be the best you can be in your own job. Be brave enough to ask questions, like what schools your coworkers went to and why they recommend them (or don't). The power is in your hands. If you discover what you're capable of and what drives you, one summer or entry-level job at a time, you'll have a list of strengths, interests, and prospective programs at your beck and call to craft the life you've always dreamt of.

5.   Social Capital

While a connection in the burger industry may not sound relevant to your dream career in the music production industry, you'll be surprised. Not only could your coworkers know the people who will help you get an in for your dream job, but they also can help you as a reference, a pillar of support as you move toward your dreams, and a source of insight and wisdom on the working world.

Write down a few jobs you've thought about doing. Dream as if there were no barriers to your potential. If you haven't considered it much before, take the time to do so now. What are fields that interest you? Feel free to be as broad or as specific as you want. In these kinds of exercises, there are no wrong answers. Some ideas include childcare, health services, construction, acting, finances, social work, visual art, writing, farming, IT, video game development, forestry...the options in front of you are still endless. What would you choose if nobody held you back?

_____ _____

_____ _____

_____ _____

Out of those fields, circle the two that interest you the most. Spend about ten minutes researching the first one. What are entry level positions like? How do you make it in that field? What does an average day look like? If you chose a broad field, find some specific job titles. What skills do you need?

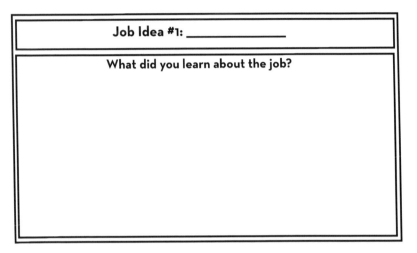

Job Idea #1: _____

What did you learn about the job?

After you spend ten minutes researching the first one you circled, repeat with the second field.

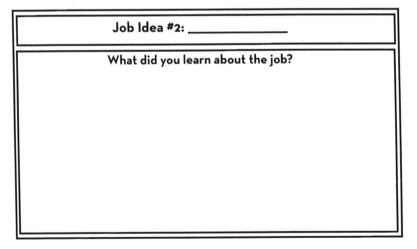

Job Idea #2: _____

What did you learn about the job?

Next, find one person - it can be someone you know, like a teacher at your school in that department - and ask them about what called them to their field. Why do they do what they do?

Job Idea #1: (_____)	
Person you talked to about the job:	
Contact Info:	
Why do they do what they do?	

Repeat for the second field you chose:

Job Idea #2: (_____)	
Person you talked to about the job:	
Contact Info:	
Why do they do what they do?	

Getting a summer job can help you determine if those two fields are the right fit for you. So don't sleep on your dreams.

Get started now.
What's one thing you can do today to help land a summer job that will help you build FEO and get you one step closer to your goals?

Ch 3: Are you ready for a summer job?

Now that we've started working through the basics of your summer job program search, you've probably started to see that there's a lot of prep work that goes into landing a spot at your ideal program - and that there may not be as many options as you'd thought. Remember that these jobs you're getting for the summer aren't the ones that you'll have for the rest of your life - it's a foundation to your FEO, the first building block to crafting the life of your dreams.

Hopefully, even just deciding to make this change has you excited by the potential for your summer: a little cash, something for your resume, maybe even a rebooted social life with similarly driven friends. But if you're sitting here thinking you can show up on day one of your job ready to roll, you're in for a surprise. There are many moving pieces in play that you're in control of to ensure you're prepped for that critical first day - and every day that follows.

It's entirely possible that this summer job is the first employment you've ever had - and that's totally okay. But even though you're new to the world of work, you have to head in with a clear idea of where you stand, as well as where you'd like to go. In the last chapter, we touched on the five elements of FEO-growth that you get from a summer job, and we'll get more in-depth later, but for now, think about these questions in the most general sense.

Let's Get to Work!		
What are some responsibilities you've had?	What are some skills you think you have?	In what ways do you think you're reliable?

So how ready do you think you are for a summer job? On a scale of one to ten, where one is "I can't even picture myself at a job ever" and ten is "I've never been more ready for something in my life," jot down a quick number here:

_____

With that number in hand, think back to the exercise at the beginning of the book, where we looked at your life one year from this moment, after you've completed the summer job program. Look to the more immediate future, just six months from now, and ask yourself this: What do you need to do now to improve your economic opportunities six months down the line?

_____

_____

_____

Do you have a vision for how to go about that yet? If you only have a vague idea, don't worry. This book will get you lined up and poised for success with the help of your summer job program. If you're looking to make the biggest splash in your life and really turn things around in six months, consider this:

What do you do that lets people around you know you're serious about working?

_____

_____

_____

_____

By knowing where you stand, you give yourself a better idea of where you're starting from and how to move forward from there. Take this quick quiz to check in with how prepared you really are for the job you're heading out to do – but remember! Quizzes are only effective if you're honest with yourself. The more transparently you answer, the better an idea you'll have of what you need to get out of the summer job program. At this stage in your journey, there are no wrong answers – each answer here leads you to your best life and greatest FEO.

For each of these questions, rank yourself using this scale.				
1	2	3	4	5
My actions and attitudes show this is never true.	My actions and attitudes show this is almost never true.	My actions and attitudes show this is some-times true.	My actions and attitudes show this is often true.	My actions and attitudes show this is always true.

1. I'm willing and able to show up to work consistently and on time. _____

Why did you choose that number? _____
_____

Describe a time when you've demonstrated this ability at work, school, or in your community:

_____

_____

What can you do to move one number up the scale?

_____

2. I'm willing and able to follow directions. _____
Why did you choose that number?

_____

Describe a time when you've demonstrated this ability at work, school, or in your community:

_____

_____

What can you do to move one number up the scale?

_____

_____

3. I'm willing and able to be trustworthy. _____
Why did you choose that number?

_____ _____

Describe a time when you've demonstrated this ability at work, school, or in your community:

_____

_____

What can you do to move one number up the scale?

_____

4. I'm willing and able to show up looking professional and with a good attitude. _____
Why did you choose that number?

____ ____ _____

Describe a time when you've demonstrated this ability at work, school, or in your community:

_____

_____

What can you do to move one number up the scale?

_____ ____ ____

5. I'm willing and able to be alcohol and drug-free. ____ __
Why did you choose that number?

Describe a time when you've demonstrated this ability at work, school, or in your community:

_____

_____

_____

What can you do to move one number up the scale?

_____

6. I am willing and able to handle my paycheck responsibly.

_____

Why did you choose that number?

Describe a time when you've demonstrated this ability at work, school, or in your community:

_____

_____

_____

What can you do to move one number up the scale?

_____

7. I am willing and able to complete high school. If I've left high school, I'm willing and able to obtain my GED. _____ __

Why did you choose that number?

_____

Describe a time when you've demonstrated this ability at work, school, or in your community:

_____

_____

_____

What can you do to move one number up the scale?

_____

8. I am willing and able to work positively and effectively with others. _____

Why did you choose that number?

_____

Describe a time when you've demonstrated this ability at work, school, or in your community:

_____

_____

_____

What can you do to move one number up the scale?

_____

Look over all your answers and write down the average of all the scores you gave yourself. To do that, add up each answer, and divide by the number of questions (eight).

_____ _____ (total of all your answers) / 8 (the total number of questions) = _____

The answer you get is your actual readiness on a scale of 1 to 5. If you're better off than you thought, then congratulations! Just remember there's always room to improve. If you're disappointed to see your average so low, just think about the future and what you can do to make those changes. You have the ability to embody all the shifts you wrote down above to help you move one number (or more!) up the scale. For now, choose two things from above, and commit to the changes by writing them below.

To get those changes going, the baby steps I'll take today are:
1
2

> **Today, I'll start building my FEO by committing to these two changes:**
>
> 1
>
> 2

When you make these changes, you'll be surprised by how easily everything else falls into place. Playing your cards right by being prepped for everything a summer job will throw your way not only makes your next few weeks brighter, but also gives you the opportunity to kickstart your future. If you feel stressed by how many things you have on your plate to change, don't let it get to you: just like how bad things snowball and seem to pile on each other, the same happens with good things: the more effort you put into pushing for your FEO, the easier all other aspects become and the more like second nature the good stuff gets.

And you don't have to do this alone. Who is one adult in your life that can serve as a mentor to help you navigate the ins and outs of summer job success? This can be an instructor guiding you through this book, a supportive family member, or your supervisor on the job site.

_____

Reach out to the person you wrote down and share with them the places you realized you need to improve, and the two baby steps you've written down for success. Be receptive to any advice they have for how to better achieve those goals. What did they recommend?

_____

_____

_____

Ch 4: Applying for a Summer Job

If you're reading this now, then there's a chance you're already all enrolled in a summer job program and are simply looking to make the most of those next few weeks you have ahead. If so, then great! But if not, it's time to get hustling to make sure you're maximizing your summer opportunities. If there's still time, get applying to a summer job program as soon as possible.

To snag a summer job, you could go out there and bubble in resumes at every shop in a strip mall, day in and day out until someone bites, but that gets tedious – fast – and is a less-than reliable method for yielding results. Instead, dive into the job search armed with knowledge to help you make the most of your time. There are many different avenues for finding a job.

Did you know that social capital is the number one way to find a job? According to a 2012 survey, connections are leaps and bounds more effective than job boards like Craigslist, LinkedIn or Indeed: 46% of people get jobs through who they know, while only 20% found jobs through job boards – and only 14% landed them through job agencies4. That means you should be putting energy into job-hunting the same way: spend half of all your time looking by reaching out to people you know and asking if they know about any openings or have any career insight. When you have people in your corner who see you're serious about looking, they're using their brainpower and web of connections to help you get that job, broadening the scope of your search well beyond what you could find just stomping the pavement. Before you start working your way through strip malls and applying to random jobs consider how your social capital could help you out.

Who can you reach out to about a summer job?

Let's get to work!			
Who can you reach out to about a summer job?	What's their contact info?	Where do they work?	Why are they a good connection to ask?

Build a Hub

If you're serious about landing a summer job - and even more serious about making sure your summer job is an experience that builds up your FEO - gather a group of people who are supportive and willing to help you out. Those people are called your "hub." The average person has around 611 connections...who each have 611 connections, giving you a network of almost 400,000 people. That's 400,000 connections you could be making. Mind blown? The trouble is, what can you even do with that many contacts? Short of reaching out to three hundred people a day for over three years, you'll never connect with them all. Instead of spamming everyone with emails and calls for years to come, hold this incredible network in your mind and realize that your potential for connecting is immense.

To make your connections count, you have to be smart about who you're reaching out to. According to the Dunbar's Number theory[5], our brains can only handle meaningful connections with about 150 people - five of which serve as your inner circle. And that means it's not about the quantity of connections you make; it's the quality. And to maximize your success, your hub members have gotta be top notch. Airports are a kind of hub: they're major points that help you get from one part of the country (or world) to another, without having to drive yourself through each connecting point between. Without these hubs, travel would be a nightmare. Hubs are efficient, saving you time and resources and letting you arrive at your destination as quickly as possible. Your social hub is no different. It's there to connect you to your goals with the least amount of shuffling in between. That's why who is in your hub is critical: why choose someone who can only move you one step in the right direction when you know someone who can move you up three?

The power of connections is vast, and it all depends on how you navigate the web of people in your life. You don't have to build a massive network - you have to build your hub and the value of your social capital. An ideal hub contains people who both believe in your potential and have some-thing to offer for your success. They can help you gain   information about available jobs, give you the lowdown on career opportunities, and encourage you to push yourself. These people should be your mentors, but also people you can trust as friends, who are candid and supportive, willing to share their own experiences, and accept you as you are.

Once you get going, it'll amaze you how quickly your hub comes together. Many adults are eager to positively engage in a young person's life, and more and more professionals are recognizing how powerful it is to invest in your generation. And it all starts with asking.

Find at least five adults and one successful young adult to be part of your hub. You can invite people from your church or mosque, a teacher you respect, or someone who works in your neighborhood. If coming up with five adults feels like a stretch, start by just picking one adult who can help work with you to find the other members. But don't forget about finding a young adult for your hub who is a thriving and positive influence. That young adult is key, since they're someone you can relate to on a level you may hold back from other, older hub members, and they'll be able to give you the frankest advice.

Interact with each of your hub members once a month at least in some way. Your monthly one-on-ones can take place on the phone if you can't coordinate a time to meet in person, but make sure you get some face-to-face time at least once a season. After you've spent a few months building up your relationships with each hub member, try scheduling a group call where the hub members can talk about your development – but keep it short and sweet (no more than fifteen minutes).

Each time you show up to meet with one of your hub members, don't go empty-handed, expecting to receive some secret knowledge. To make it count, just like your summer job, you have to show up prepared, or risk wasting your hub's (or boss's) time, damaging the trust and connection you've been building. Each time you meet with your hub members, discuss how your job is going and any struggles you've encountered, but also have examples of what you've accomplished since then: has your boss given you new tasks, or did you complete a program? Share it!

And beyond just sharing your accomplishments and hiccups, ask hard questions - and be as direct as possible. For exam-ple, instead of saying, "I need help finding a job that builds on my existing skills," say, "I'd like for each of you to give me the names of three individuals I can contact regarding possible employment that builds on the skills I've been working on." That directness will feel like a breath of fresh air for your hub.

Just remember: your hub members aren't robots there to just serve your growth - they're humans with feelings and thoughts and opinions, so take time to pop in for informal meetings. Visit at least two hub members monthly. Give them a call and say you'll be in the area and would like to stop by their office. When you visit, take the time to strengthen your relationship. Talk about what they do and how they're doing. Ask questions. Learn about who they are and how they got to where they are. People love the chance to open up about themselves, and by learning their story, you're strengthening the bridge between you two. If it's possible, take the time to say hi to your hub member's coworkers, laying foundations for those connections as well.

If you want your hub to work, you have to make it work. Stay in touch, call meetings to order, and be specific about your needs. This is your team - and you're in charge. If you don't put the work into making sure each meeting works for you, you won't get what you want from it.

When getting a feel for hub candidates, look for people who fill these three roles:
1. **Friends**

A good hub member has time to listen and provide compassionate advice with. They are someone who notices the little things and knows how powerful simple phrases like "I'm proud of you" are when it comes to building your self-esteem. They're someone who knows that time is needed to build a relationship – and is willing to invest that time in you.

2. Role Models

Hub members have overcome their own obstacles to enjoy their successful lives, and they're not afraid to share their past with you. This responsibility can crop up in a variety of ways. Maybe a member offers to take you to work with them one day. Maybe they're a role model through their mannerisms, even temper, or positive energy. A hub member should share their own goals and visions and always help you out when you're seeking ways to further your education and career opportunities.

3. Links to your Community and to Business

A good hub member has their finger on the pulse of the community and is bold enough to seek out any information they don't have that will help you be your best self. Hub members will need to know (or be down to learn) who the community and business resources are and how to access them, sniffing out information and developing your community business network so you can land meaningful and gainful employment.

In the space below, write down people who could be in your hub. When you call them, explain what a hub is and what the duties would entail. Moreover, share what it is you have to offer them as a driven, hopeful young person.

By creating a hub now, you're creating a safety net of folks who genuinely have your best interest in mind and will show you the way to be a successful and thriving young adult in the working world.

Who will you contact for your hub?					
Who could be part of your hub?					
How can you help them?					
How can they help you?					
What industry do they work in?					
What's their contact info?					
When will you reach out?					

Stay Organized

Ask anyone in the job-hunting game, and they'll be quick to tell you that applying to jobs is and should be a full-time job. To make it - and nail those interviews - you have to be doing active work daily to get the most out of your time. Be careful, though - there's a big difference between working a ton and working smart. By keeping organized, you can spare yourself a lot of headaches and anxiety while still landing the job you seek.

It can be overwhelming to wake up in the morning and see "get a job" on your to-do list. When you give yourself such an open-ended task, it feels impossible to know where to start. But if you break that mountain-sized task into smaller pieces, it goes from feeling impossible to looking manageable. Follow the path of thousands of successful people before you to avoid the trap of too-large tasks: make a schedule. All successful people have a schedule they follow, whether they're your biology teacher or Beyoncé - and that's exactly what you need to do as you hunt for the right job to help you build up your FEO.

Instead of having a to-do list that just says "get a job," think about seven tasks you can complete today to work toward that goal. Think achievable. Maybe one task is simply writing a list of places to apply. Another task can be finding one volunteer opportunity in walking distance. Get started now! Here's a sampling from a schedule that a successful job seeker may have:

8:00 - wake up
8:00-8:30 - brush teeth, get ready, eat breakfast
8:30-8:45 - write down three jobs I want, then google articles on how to be great at these jobs
8:45-9:00 - ID three companies with jobs in that field

And that's all just to get their day started. Write down your own schedule for tomorrow to help you get as much done as possible to land that job. Fill out at least ten things to do and the times you'll do them to maximize the hours in your day. When you build your schedule, remember to include any appointments or plans you've already made, so you aren't caught off guard tomorrow.

_:_ - _____

_:_ - _____

_:_ - _____

_:_ - _____

_:_ - _____

_:_ - _____

_:_ - _____

_:_ - _____

_:_ - _____

_:_ - _____

Tomorrow morning, don't hesitate. Follow this schedule and see what happens. By working smart, you'll be unlocking potential for your goals to bear that fruit.

Don't Wait for the Cheddar to Start Building Connections
Don't snooze on opportunity just because you can't find something that gives you cash just yet. If you're applying to jobs and nothing's panned out, sign up to volunteer somewhere that interests you. Getting your foot in the door as a volunteer is a wonderful way to gain experience, put something on your resume, and connect with adults who see you as driven and responsible. With those perks and knowledge under your belt, you won't be unemployed for long. And through volunteer work, you may have access to honing more high-end skills than a paying job could offer, opening you up to greater potential down the road than you thought possible – and sooner than you thought.

Get started now. Write down five skills that you're interested in developing:

_____

_____

_____

_____

_____

Next, spend at least fifteen minutes googling acces-sible and available volunteer opportunities in your area and write them down here:

_____

_____

_____

Do you gain any of the above skills through the volunteer opportunities listed? Draw a line between any that you think are related. Next, call all five opportunities and ask how to get started.

Opportunity?	How do you get started?

Don't wait for a paying job to call you back before you start building up experience. By getting the ball rolling as a volunteer sooner rather than later, you're guaranteed to not stay unemployed for long. Even if you're feeling desperate, volunteering is the key to building up opportunities for yourself down the road and is the best way to build your resume and social capital for a long future of success and financial abun-dance. You got this. What can you do ASAP to build your resume?

_____

_____

Ch 5: More than a Paycheck

Your summer job or program is more than just a chance to score some summer cash you can stash away for a rainy day. These are your FEO-building years, the time when you lay groundwork for your economic prosperity down the line. Think about it - the sooner you start building a foundation, the more quickly you can get that high rise off the round. Rome wasn't built in a day, and neither is a successful and financially rich future. Diving into a summer work experience, dedicated to your own future, is the best way to lock in on these five facets of your own FEO and get started on building them up. We gave you the short version in Chapter Two, but here's the run down on the five, and some questions to get you thinking in depth:

1.   Work Experience

The most obvious perk of a summer job program is the experience itself. Getting work under your belt is key to landing better-paying jobs with opportunities for career growth down the road. Nothing is more daunting than a blank application and no experience to fill it with. By getting into a program and starting the work, you're starting out on a long line of success ahead - as long as you make the most of it. It's not just clock-ing in that'll pave the way for you; while you're at work, you have to put effort in, learn the tasks, and be an employee that your supervisors will be happy to give references for in the future. One of the biggest pitfalls of young people entering the job market is that they have had jobs but blew their work experience by quitting on a dime or getting fired because they didn't do their work. Keep record of new skills you learn - you should be acquiring two every thirty days - and show up when you say you will.

One of the easiest ways to make sure you're actually gaining worthwhile experience and not just wasting your time? Ask. Approach your summer job supervisor and ask them about the best ways to maximize your experience and areas of improvement. The people you work for will be more than happy to offer advice, cross-training, or insight on the different facets of the job, opening you up to a whole other realm of experience. Give it a try. At your next shift, ask your supervisor what they recommend you do to make the most of your work experience. If you haven't started yet, be sure to ask them for advice week one, so you don't miss out on anything. Write down what you learn in the space below.

_____

_____

_____

Put that advice to action next time you go in to work. What did you do? How did it go? What insight did you gain from trying their suggestion?

_____

_____

_____

_____

_____

2.   Connections

The next time you're on the clock, take a good look at the coworkers and supervisors around you. That crew makes up the key players influencing your future career ladder pivots – at least until you land the next big job. For better or worse, the connections you make now are the ones that have the power to rattle the structure of your life and opportunities.

A mistake many young people make is leaving a bad impression at their first job. By showing up to work with a stink face and a salty attitude, clocking in late, or being rude to customers, you're negatively impacting your future career chances. By having a positive attitude, you can get the job done without leaving a bad taste in your boss's mouth when they think about you.

However, there's a less talked about mistake, one just as glaring, that even more young people make at their first job: failing to make an impression at all. Don't invest your energy in staying under the radar and scraping by doing only what's been asked. By doing so, you're missing out on the opportunity to build up a stellar network of connections who are wowed by your performance - and subsequently an enthusiastic support system in your corner down the line.

Take the plunge. Go from being a forgettable employee (or a downright bad one) to a knockout one. Reach out to the older folks in your job or program. Ask them everything they can about their experiences on the job. You'll be amazed by the wide insight and wisdom they have just lying around and are more than willing to share with young people eager to get a head start. Remember to be kind and open. Smile. Take a genuine interest in listening to what they have to say and build a human connection. Nothing feels worse than talking to someone who's using you as a tool or a ladder rung and only has half an ear on the conversation.

Get started as soon as possible. At your next shift, approach someone who's been working that position for much longer than you - try several years longer - or is significantly older. Ask them about their experience in the workforce and at the company, and how to succeed in that position. Try asking these questions and write down what you learn in the space below each:

What's the thing you've learned the most since you started working here?

_____

_____

What was the hardest thing for you starting out?

_____

_____

What do you wish someone had told you your first month here?

_____

_____

What're your favorite and least favorite things about the job?

_____

_____

Any advice for me?

_____

_____

Reflect on what they told you, and don't let it just go in one ear and out the other. How does their wisdom impact your future career choices and the rest of your time at this summer job?

_____

_____

Connections don't have to be limited to people well up the ladder. Every job you apply for for the rest of your life, no matter if you're at a senior level or shifting into entry-level work at a new field, you will be asked for professional references. Show yourself to be a hardworking and friendly coworker to the peers who have as much experience as you do, and ask them explicitly if you can be each other's professional references down the line. Exchange contact information and tell them about your journey with this book. As young peo-ple starting out, you are stronger together making the right choices. By being the person that offers your peers more information and an opportunity to grow, you are helping others in ways you may not have known you were capable of. These connections you make with peers can serve you as you both navigate new jobs down the road: if you've proven yourself as a reliable coworker, these peers will be more likely to recommend you apply to whatever new job they get when there's an opening.

If you do all this, you'll be hungry for more. Check out www. edwarddejesus.com and join the MAKiN' iT Nation and follow the hashtag #makinitnation to keep up with the growing culture of social capital building for young people everywhere, and build community with your peers to get started sooner rather than later. Through this all, keep referring back to the hub you've built. Deepen your existing connections as you find new ones.

3.   Credentials

Credentials are another crucial aspect of the summer jobs program. They're the certifications, paperwork, and official signifiers of having completed a program, mastered a skill, or studied a topic. If you're involved in a summer job program, you could be earning a credential through the program. But even if the program you're in doesn't offer a credential, your job program is a prime opportunity to get the inside scoop on the best credentials for you - straight from the mouths of people who've received the credentials. Use your hub, your supervisors, and anyone else you've reached out to over the course of this book to find out where the reputable programs are. And if you work hard in your summer program, don't be afraid to ask about opportunities for the company itself to sponsor a credential. People often don't know what it is you want, but once you open up and tell them, they'd be more than happy to help you get there.

What are three career paths that interest you? It can be as vague as "science" or as specific as "sushi chef." Beside each career, write down the name and number of someone who is skilled in that field that you know. If you don't know someone, look up their information.

_____/_____/_____

_____/_____/_____

_____/_____/_____

Then, contact those people and ask them the questions below, writing their answers in the space provided.

Let's get to work!	
What credentials will help you secure an entry-level position in this industry?	Where should you go to get the credential and is there enrollment assistance?
1	1
	2
2	1
	2
3	1
	2

If your summer job is related to the career that interests you, ask your coworkers and supervisors about their credentials for the best insight into that field. Even if you're working in an ice cream parlor and want to get involved in nonprofit fundraising, ask your bosses about their credentials. By learning the ins and outs of where you currently are, you'll gain a unique perspective on where it is you want to go. What kinds of credentials do your supervisors have?

_____

What credentials do they recommend for becoming the best you can be in the path you're both on now?

_____

4. Education

On all applications you fill out, someone is going to ask about your education. Getting your high school diploma is crucial if you want to get ahead in life. Not having one - even getting a GED instead - can negatively affect your future economic opportunity greatly. All too often, students are given a cookie cutter education that doesn't work for everyone. Stuck with binary options, like getting a four-year degree or not getting a degree at all, excludes the possibility of other ways to learn. But have you ever considered other methods of education?

Instead of a four-year or even two-year program, think creatively about your passions. Curious about becoming a personal trainer? Start looking into training programs. Want to be a visual artist or potter? Take classes at a rec center or reach out to artists to learn under them in exchange for studio help. Education is constantly evolving, and any classes you take are worth sharing with prospective employers, especially if you complete the program offered.

By now in this book you should be honing an idea of the job you want in the long haul. Who can you reach out to and talk about it? _____
Ask this person all about their education - what helped them get to where they are?

What education do they recommend?

What's the best place to get started?

What do they wish they'd known when they were starting out?

If you can, ask your summer job advisor for any advice on education in the field that interests you. Write it down below:

5.   Skills

No matter what job you land for the summer, you have the opportunity to learn valuable skills. Although when we think of skills, we frequently jump to things like "how to cook rice" or "how to use Powerpoint", those are only half the types of skills you can learn – those are called "hard skills." Hard skills are objective and direct to teach. You can get them through formal training or education to perform specific work. Examples include science, math, writing, engineering, language, and sewing.

Soft skills, on the other hand, are interpersonal qualities better known as "people skills." These are the things like work ethic, communication, etiquette, time management, and problem-solving. Soft skills are all about your ability to be a team player, keep a positive attitude, work well under pressure, and manage constructive criticism. Often, soft skills are written off as personality traits (and therefore unlearnable), but soft skills in truth are things you have the power to master, like any other skill.

Regardless of the job you're looking for, soft and hard skills are a must. Employers aren't just looking for one or the other. They're looking for the whole package – which can be you. If you want to stand out from the pack, you have to work on developing "essential" skills. A good method is the 2/1/30 rule: learn two new skills and one new habit every thirty days. If you put that to practice in your summer job program, you could be looking at 2.2 new skills in that time alone.

Learn some skills on the job. The best way to do that? Speak up! One of the primary ways to maximize your time in your summer job or program is simply by asking for more tasks and challenges. Often, employers have no idea that you're looking to push yourself and be the best you can be. Don't be another rank and file young employee who passively lets opportunity pass them by.

On your next shift, approach your supervisor and ask them these questions, writing their answers in the space below:

"What's the number one skill I can learn on the job that will help me get ahead down the road?"

_____

"What do I have to do to get started?"

_____

They'll be impressed by your drive and motivated by your attitude. By taking a vested interest in your time you spend at work, you'll be equipped with skills that help you land that next, more challenging, better-paying job down the line.

Ch 6: ...but let's not forget the paycheck altogether

The five facets of opportunity that come from your summer job program help lay out the tools you need to land bigger paychecks down the line, really unlocking your freedom and potential. By laying that groundwork now, you're setting yourself up for the most success, abundance, and happiness your life can muster. But does that necessarily mean you should close your eyes to all the money coming in from this first job now? No way.

That money coming in now is another learning opportunity. Most summer jobs and summer job programs pay minimum wage. While you won't exactly be raking in the dollars just yet with these early paychecks, you will be dealing with a legitimate cash flow – more than you likely have had before. These are some of the common ways young people blow their first few paychecks:

1. Booze or drugs
2. Sneaker game
3. Take out
4. Fashion brands
5. Tattoos
6. Lotto tickets/Scratch-offs
7. Boyfriend/Girlfriend/Other
8. Concerts
9. Weapons

We get it. When you have a check made out in your name with several hundred dollars on it, you may be tempted to blow it all on shoes, lunch, a new look, or some tattoos, but not so fast. By saving what you get and continuing to be mindful of where that money's going, you're setting yourself up for more financial freedom in the long run, empowering you to enjoy some of the things in that list above (and then some) when you land that first well-paying job. And if you're ready for that, you won't be caught off guard when it comes time to be paying your own bills.

If you don't know how to plan, the effects can be detrimental. Look at people who land a record deal, modeling contract, or pro ball position and think they're set for life...until they go and blow that money on a yacht, a mansion, and beachside vacations, only to find themselves forty years old and broker than a joke.

Most people don't earn anywhere near what those folks get in their contracts, so you need to be just as careful (if not more) to make sure you're smart with your money. First off, let's check in on how much money you actually have outgoing or will have if you go after all the things that you want to get:

An Honest Budget			
Hobbies:		Helping the family:	
Activities:		Savings:	
Phone:		Clothes:	
Transportation (bus, car payments, etc.):		_____:	
Restaurants:		_____:	
Extra groceries:		_____:	
	Total Expenses:	_____:	

Surprised by how much money that adds up to each month? By being smart now, you'll make a difference down the line once you start paying your own bills.

Money Drains

If you're clocking in and just showing up to do the bare minimum to earn those dollars, you'll be in for a surprise down the line: scraping by is going to leave you and the people you work for scraping for quarters in the long run.

How? When it comes to the employer, for each minute you spend not working, they're going to have to pay you to stand around and text, and your coworker to do the job you're supposed to be doing. This strains businesses and makes them have to find an employee who will do the job they've been assigned sooner rather than later. And the lack of productivity on your end really adds up for companies – especially mom and pop shops:

Situation	A: Hourly Wage	B: Wage by the Minute (divide amount in A by 60)	C: Cost of unproductivity (multiply B by number of minutes in situation	Cost of unproductivity if 4 employees do this every day for a year (multiply C by 4 and then by 365)
Ex: A fast food worker spends 5 minutes on her phone	$10.00	$0.16	$0.85	$1216.67
#1: A mechanic shows up 15 minutes late	$25.00			
#2: A grocery clerk bags so slowly he loses 12 minutes an hour	$9.50			
#3: A delivery driver stops at a friend's house for 10 minutes	$12.00			

You may be wondering why you should care about costing an employer a few dollars. You, after all, are still getting yours. If you're in a subsidized program, you may even feel like it's not their money – it's Uncle Sam's. Not so fast. These indirect costs can hurt your employer with wasted supervision, squandered resources, strained staff relationships...and it hurts you just as much with lost connections, promotions, references, and learning or skill-building opportunities. And if you're in an unsubsidized program, then your poor work ethic directly impacts your employers financially. Your employer notices if you aren't doing what you're supposed to, and that lack of drive impacts the future that helps you fund all the things in the budget you created above - and beyond. And if you're breaking into the tip-based industry - think servers, bartenders, baristas, and performers - your customers will notice if you're on your phone, ignoring them, and not valuing their time as well as yours, and will tip you accordingly.

If you fail to show up on time, complete your tasks, and be an employee worth hiring, you could be slowly building the case for you to lose your job before the summer program finishes. Calling in late or absent in an actual emergency is fine - that's what time off is for. But if you're strolling in late after going out to lunch or taking a sick day to head to the movies, it puts you on the chopping block down the line. And if you show up as an employee who costs more than they contribute, you could be spoiling opportunities for other young people down the line by making your employer hesitant to give young people a chance through a summer program again. Don't be the reason others (and you!) lose your chance.

The easiest thing you can do? Work when you say you will. Show up when you're scheduled. Do your tasks and ask for something else to do when you finish. These small changes will revolutionize your future.

	give examples of how those in the previous **chart** should **maximize their time**
#1:	
#2:	
#3:	

Since these hours you maximize (or don't) add up on future paychecks down the line, you have to ensure you get the best summer work experience possible that leads you to good connections and skills. Otherwise, your work experience and attitude wastes both your own time and your employer's.

By embracing productivity and dedication to doing the right thing to make it, you'll be building a lot of future opportunities. But beware: when you're productive, an employer will want you to work more, and may offer you all sorts of perks and incentives to get there. But you need to make sure your working hours stay at or under fifteen each week: remember, there are five facets of FEO, and two of them are your credentials and education. Turn down the extra hours they offer, no matter how enticing quick money is, and invest those hours in your future instead. And if, after several months or the end of the summer, you need to focus on your education or move on to a program that pushes your skillset further, don't be afraid to pass promotions or offers by. Just always make sure you move forward with a reference in hand, at least two skills you've mastered, and a solid track record for attendance and reliability.

Work starts with you, and so does your future. Showing up and scraping by with the bare minimum won't get you very far, so why waste time doing that? Instead, give your best version of yourself every single day. When the work is done, instead of hanging out with your friends and sharing a cigarette out back, find your supervisor and ask what else can be done. Organize the work van or wipe down counters. Put things away. Read the manual. By being someone your employer is sure to remember as a driven and motivated employee, you're paving the road for both acquiring the most skills possible and being on good terms with someone who can serve as a reference as your career grows.

When you are an employee worth noticing, you are inviting raises, long-term employment opportunities, and other benefits, as well as giving you a better sense of the job you're part of and all it entails. Like we discussed in chapter two, the worst outcome is that you'll realize this field isn't for you and be able to move on to another job next summer. By giving a position your all, you quickly learn the ins and outs, discover your favorite and least favorite aspects, and are better equipped to shift into a position that aligns with what you love.

If you've already started your summer job program, write down three things you can do during your next shift to help you stand out from the crowd as a productive team member:

1. _____

2. _____

3. _____

If you haven't started yet, what are some things you can do your first week to show that you're a productive member of the crew who's serious about their success?
1. _____
2. _____
3. _____

By planning ahead, triple-checking your schedule, putting the phone down, and saving some money, you're laying the groundwork for an abundant and financially rich future. You got this.

Ch 7: How to Be Successful in Your Summer Job

So maybe by now you've landed a summer job, or are at least in the final throes of an interview process. Congratulations! Now it's time to start thinking about the best ways to be a stellar employee. You've already reflected on your time management and opportunities for building social capital, but there are a few key rules of thumb for getting there in the first place.

It all Starts with Motivation

Consistently working on your FEO is hard work. Some-times, you may feel drawn to the path of least resistance, falling into traps that give you a quick turnaround while putting your life, freedom, and FEO at risk. We'll level with you: if being a success was easy, everyone would be jumping on board. The truth is, success requires discipline, hard work, and laser focus. In order to develop that single-mindedness, you have to be motivated.

The big question is, where does that motivation come from? Often, our society hones in on external motivators like peer pressure, wanting something fancy, or hoping to make your loved ones proud. But real motivation, the kind that lasts through all kinds of weather, comes from inside. It's called intrinsic motivation. Intrinsically motivated people undertake an activity or job for its own sake, the learning it makes way for, or the feelings of accomplishment the work itself awakens. In contrast, external factors are called extrinsic motivation and they push someone to do a task so they can get a reward or avoid a punishment separate from the activity itself – think money, new kicks, or bragging rights. The problem with extrinsic motivators is that they run out. The new kicks get scuffed, money drains to pay the bills, and soon your friends will all have jobs too. Intrinsic motivations keep you going when the extrinsic ones lose their shine.

Here are some reasons why people attend work regularly. Look them over and mark "I" for actions that seem intrinsic, and "E" for those that are extrinsic.

___ I would like to learn new things.
___ I pay rent because my mother is making me.
___ My father does not want me to sit around at home doing nothing.
___ I need money to pay my car insurance.
___ I would like to work where my friends work.
___ I would like to learn to use new tools.
___ I would like the self-satisfaction.
___ I would like to work because I have non money.
___ I would like the satisfaction of accomplishment.
___ I would like to support myself.
___ I would like to get new clothes.
___ I would like to buy a car.
___ I would like to stay busy and not be bored.

Why do you think it is that some people are more extrinsically motivated?

_____

_____

Who do you know that's intrinsically motivated? What do they do? Why do they do it?

_____

_____

_____

Whatever that person has in their life that inspires them to be intrinsically motivated can be nurtured in your own life too. Maybe you need to pursue something that motivates you, or work toward a broader goal in building your FEO.

What is one thing you can do to make yourself more intrinsically motivated?

_____

_____

Intrinsic motivation helps you keep going when those extrinsic motivators are missing. Work isn't always glamorous. There won't always be someone reminding you to do something, or a looming punishment. By expecting external motivators to push you toward the right track, you set yourself up for a line of disappointment. By moving through life already as an extrinsically-motivated individual, you've lost opportunities that may have otherwise changed your life. What is something you've personally lost because of a lack of motivation?

_____

_____

If you keep on this track of no motivation, where do you see yourself in five years?

_____

_____

What if you were motivated by your own internal capability, your own drive? What do you think you'd be capable of then? How would the vision of your future look different five years from now?

_____

_____

This isn't to say extrinsic motivators are totally without value. There are plenty of valid things you want to work toward. A healthy balance of the internal and the external is key to making the most of your summer job.

What is something extrinsic you want to achieve in the next twelve months? It could be anything from making your mother proud to buying the latest Nikes.

_____

_____

What about something intrinsic? A skill you want to learn, or something you want from yourself?

_____

_____

What are two things you can do at your next shift to start working towards those goals?

1._____

2. _____

Shifting your mentality to foster a healthy balance of extrinsic and intrinsic motivation takes diligence, repetition, and practice. By reading this book and doing the exercises here, you've taken vital steps in the work needed to motivate yourself. Keep looking toward the future and acknowledging the work you have ahead to make your life the best it can be now. There are a million things you are capable of and can become just by having a good attitude and keeping on in your pursuit of your goals.

The Internet is a Tool, so Use It

In the United States, most of us are lucky enough to have something incredible in our purse or back pocket: a tool so powerful that it can change lives, share information, give directions, and teach new skills. I'm talking about our smart phones. Unfortunately, most people don't act like it, instead gobbling up social media feeds and new music while scratching their heads about how to stand out, make that green, and be a knockout.

Social media can be a wonderful way to keep in touch with friends and family. All too often, however, people get ad-dicted, losing themselves in the glamour and glitz of celebrity profiles or influencers who seem to be living one long string of parties. Music, Instagram, magazine, and videos lead peo-ple on, keeping them trapped in the delusion that you can be a star by living life as an endless music festival. In reality, these celebrities have put in long hours, cancelled countless plans, and worked many a long night to get to the point they are now, and even once they've made it, they spend their days hard at work, staying on top. Jay-Z didn't become one of the wealthiest people in the U.S. by partying every day, and you won't either. What's the most insidious thing about social media is that folks don't share these things, and you aren't encouraged to put in the work. It's a whole new generation of the "Keeping up with the Jones'" mentality. So instead of spending your time using the internet to share only the best parts of your life, try using it as the tool it is: engage with others that motivate you. Seek out content that talks about the work. Follow hashtags related to the industry of your dreams and get inspired to take active steps to be a success in that industry yourself.

If you're eager to find some peer support, follow and use these hashtags to get involved in the MAKiN' iT Nation and see others like you on that journey for success:

#makinitnation #opportunitysummer #makinit

To make the most of your job and your summer, recognize the internet as the powerful tool it is, offering you so much more than just a way to show off to your friends or serve your fiercest angles. It's a way to learn. If you don't know a skill, Google it. If you want tips on how to do your best at your job, check our brother Yo'utu-be. His government name is YouTube. You'll be amazed to see the incredible amount of information that already exists to help you navigate any aspect of your job or ambitions.

The best way to be a success in the workplace is to stop subscribing to the negative feedback on the media that keeps you away from positive habits, the drive to acquire skills, or the full potential you have. You've got the internet at your fingertips. YouTube will show you how to make it in any field out there.

What is the career you're most interested in? Remember, dream big!

_____

Take some time now to find one YouTuber who has tips on succeeding in that career. Subscribe to them and write their name down here: _____
Watch a few of their videos and write down at least two tips they have for succeeding in your dream career:
1. _____
2. _____

Next, go to Instagram, if you have it, and follow three hashtags related to your ideal career. What hashtags are they?
1. _____
2. _____
3. _____
Finally, spend a few minutes googling the best advice for being a success in your current job. What are the most interesting pieces of advice you found?

1. _____

2. _____

What is one thing you can do at your next shift to bring you to the next level, that you learned during your time online just now?

_____

_____

The internet is powerful and full of opportunities for you to make the most of your summer program – and beyond. Keep in mind the potential of the web when you start looking for programs, schools, or new skills to acquire as you move past high school and into the next stages of your life. If you're going through it, chances are someone else has come out the other end of it before you.

Look the Part

Dressing to impress is something often learned all too late, but wearing clothes that suit the role you're showing up for goes a long way in getting ahead in those next steps.

Times are evolving; a nose ring or tattoo no longer negates your employability, and a wider diversity of aesthetics and identities are welcomed in the work force. However, just because the working world has moved its mentality into the twenty-first century, doesn't mean you can show up to work wearing exactly whatever you want. Basic rules of hygiene, appropriateness, and tidiness apply to all looks in the ever-evolving working world, and how neatly you present yourself still strongly informs whether you'll land those strong connections and be received as a valuable professional.

At their most basic, these rules revolve largely around your personal hygiene. Brush your teeth and rinse your face every morning before going in, and make sure your hair and clothes are clean and smell fresh. Avoid body odor, but at the same time, make sure you're not doused in Axe body spray or a candied perfume; strong scents can be just as detracting from your professional appearance as bad BO.

In the same vein, always keep your appearance neat. Opt for the pants without holes in them, and shirts without offensive or crude slogans. Moreover, make sure your clothes are practical for the job. If you aren't sure about the best look, button downs, sweaters, and blouses are all easy ways to look sharp without going in for a full suit jacket and tie, or if a polo shirt just isn't your thing. You don't have to don the khakis of twenty years ago, and nowadays there is a huge intersection where 'professional' and 'fashionable' meet. Just keep things sharp, and avoid clothes that show your belly or underwear, or clothes you bought with the intention of partying, exercising, or lounging around the house binging Netflix.

It boils down to staying smart, washing your hair, and finding how your own sense of style translates to the profes-sional world. If you're at a loss, a button-down paired with pants or a skirt is never the wrong choice. If you're in a job or program that has uniforms, consider yourself lucky! All you have to remember is to keep up with your personal hygiene and make sure you always have a clean uniform, so you never find yourself in a bind on the morning of a shift.

So how do you stack up in your appearance? Are you ready for that job?

Answer each question below using "N" for Never, "S" for Sometimes, and "A" for Always, depending on how well you take care of your appearance every day.
1. Do I keep my body clean? _____

2. Do I take a frequent shower or bath? _____
3. Do I clean and trim my nails? _____
4. Do I use a deodorant? _____
5. Is my hair neat and combed in private? _____
6. Is my hair washed weekly or more often? _____
7. Do I brush my teeth daily? _____
8. Do I visit the dentist every 6 months? _____
9. Do I have a yearly medical check-up? _____
10. Do I eat a balanced diet? _____
11. Do I stand and sit straight? _____
12. Are my clothes neat, clean, and mended?

_____
13. Are my shoes clean and polished? _____
14. Do I dress right for the event? _____
15. Most importantly, do I like myself? _____

In two sentences, how would you sum up your own personal style and appearance?

_____

_____

What changes, if any, would you make to your own appearance? What is a change you can take on now?

_____

_____

You've Gotta Talk the Talk, Too

Now that you look the part, people are going to start asking you questions, treating you like someone who knows the ropes and can help them out. A critical part of making it in your summer job is being able to express yourself one-on-one and in groups. At times, you may even be called on to speak in front of a large group of people. While the thought of public speaking terrifies most of us, it is a skill that is honed with practice, same as flipping a pancake or tying a tie.

To get a leg up as a public speaker, follow tips from the pros.

Someone who's good at rallying a group with their words is a meticulous planner, researcher, and rehearser. They know what they'll say, have the facts to back them up, and prac-tice in front of the mirror, their significant other, or on their phone camera. More than just planning, a good public speaker knows how to think on their feet and maintain composure when the unexpected inevitably happens.

Take this balance with you to your first day on the job. Suddenly, you may find yourself overwhelmed by the af-ter-work rush, everyone scrambling to buy things, telling you what to do, asking you difficult questions. It may be a knee-jerk reaction to get salty or turn up your stink face, but hold back for a minute. Your employers catch wind of your neg-ative reactions and they can impact your opportunities and references. Instead, try non-inflammatory communication and a smooth brow, letting your chill and positivity serve as pillars to your success on the job.

Instead of asking "why" questions when you disagree or don't understand or rolling your eyes, opt for less aggressive and clear communication. Often, a customer doesn't realize they're being rude. They're human too, and may have had a bad day. While you're helping them out, ask open-end-ed questions like, "How's your day going?"

What is something you tend to say when you're annoyed?

_____

_____

What could you say instead that doesn't start drama?

_____

_____

The only way to avoid drama is to make sure you never start it in the first place. Look, we'll tell you straight: you won't like everyone you ever meet - and everyone you ever meet won't like you. And that's okay. You don't have to be best friends with every coworker or change the life of each customer. What you do need to do, however, is exercise civility if you hope to translate your work experience to meaningful opportunity and income down the line. So instead of wondering how to get back at a coworker or assert dominance over a situation, show up as your best and most professional self, and you'll be sure to prevail in any situation thrown your way.

Avoid swearing or inflammatory language, regardless of how frustrated you may feel in a situation at work. While casual groups are fine places to swear, in a professional set-ting, leave that language at the door; you never know who you'll offend, and it's better to avoid any drama altogether by keeping your language to the kind you'd use to talk to your grandmother.

Of course, none of your words matter if you spend the whole time mumbling. Mumbling and rambling negates any important or intelligent thoughts you may be sharing with coworkers, and can aggravate customers looking for information and assistance. Speak up! Project your voice as best you can by pushing air through your stomach to make sure your valuable input doesn't go unheard. You have smart and important things to say; don't let them get lost because you're too self-conscious to get loud.

Perhaps just as important as speaking up is knowing when to listen. All workplaces are collaborative by nature. The trick to being a good listener is surprisingly easy: when someone else is talking, don't plan what you're going to say next. That's it. If you're listening to someone's story or idea and your wheels are spinning on how to share your own story, then you aren't actually listening - you're just looking for an audience to appreciate you. By opening your ears up to what others have to say, you're positioning yourself to make connections and learn things that surprise you. Think about it: what's the point of a conversation at all if you already know what it is you're going to say? You may as well be talking to the mirror if that's all you want. The purpose of conversations is to engage, learn, and exchange ideas. You'll be pleasantly surprised by everything there is to learn once you open yourself up to learning from others.

Think back to a store you've gone to that has some stellar customer service. What are three reasons you think it's particularly good?

1. _____

2. _____

3. _____

How can you put these three things to work in your next shift?

Chances are you know someone who works with customers every day. Reach out to that person and ask them what the most important skills and abilities they say you need to excel in a customer-heavy job.

_____

_____

_____

On the other side of customer service, there's something called "provider service." It means the attitude you hold towards the people providing you a service. If you treat teachers, cashiers, counselors, security guards, and library attendants with respect, people notice - and they notice if you're rude, as well. Real wealth is treating other people well, regardless of which side you're on in the exchange. That respect will go a long way in having people help make things happen for you.

Working Effectively with Your Summer Work Experience Supervisor

Of course, this is all incredibly important when work-ing with your supervisor. Make a solid impression, be receptive to what they're telling you, and do the work asked of you – and then some. In your FEO-building years and beyond, there will always be someone higher than you in the chain of command. To make it and take steps to better your future economic opportunity and make a difference, getting along with your supervisor is key. And there's no better place to get started learning how to work with your bosses than at your first summer job.

Think about your experiences with authority – your parents, teachers, the law – and consider how you handled those experiences. What did you do that promoted your life, freedom, and future economic opportunity?

_____

_____

When was a time you created drama that you would have been better off avoiding?

_____

_____

Think back to the section before about communica-tion and avoiding drama – what is something you could have done in the dramatic situation above to help further your opportunities?

_____

_____

To work best with your summer job program advisor,

communicate transparently about everything, good and bad. Supervisors know you're new and learning - that's the entire point of the program, isn't it? - and so if you don't understand the task at hand, ask them explicitly to help you understand it better. They'll be glad you asked, rather than doing it wrong and having to circle back and do it all over again. What many folks don't realize is that communicating a hole in your own knowledge doesn't make employers think you're stupid - it's a learning moment for you, and a chance for them to teach you how to do things better.

Another thing about working effectively with them is to ask them for extra work once you finish. Supervisors notice if you're just hanging out on your phone. To stand out from the pack, ask to take on extra tasks - so long as you can man-age them.

Finally, communicate explicitly about any physical lim-itations you may have when it comes to completing a task. You'll be surprised by how accommodating supervisors can be when they know your needs and how to meet them best. Supervisors are there to help you be the best employee you can be - and when you ask them to light the way, you're help-ing them do their job and helping yourself succeed at the same time.

Cultural Competence: Working Effectively with People from Other Cultures

Now more than ever, we're living in a global culture. As our world grows smaller and more interwoven, it would be a costly mistake to assume you'll only be working alongside people who look, act, or present like you do. Immigration and welcoming people with open arms are cornerstones of the modern world. In your summer job experience, expect to get to know coworkers whose first language, skin color, sexual orientation, gender expression, and religion differ greatly from yours.

When you are lucky enough to meet someone in your job who is different from you, take a step back and remember not to be rude. Think before asking culturally insensitive questions or making broad assumptions about someone. Before you speak, imagine the script being flipped on you, or if someone said to you the things you are considering saying to them. What demographic do you most strongly identify with that impacts your life the most?

Think back to a time when someone said something hurtful to you about something unchangeable in your life - possibly that demographic listed above. How did you react? How did you feel?

What do you wish they'd said to you instead?

Regardless of where you're coming from, everybody wants to be treated with dignity and respect. Sometimes, that means taking a hard look at your own life and contemplating how to make changes that invite diverse people into your circle. Think to your own friends group - what demographic is totally unrepresented in the circles you run in? This can be someone's race, gender, religion, body type, sexuality, income, or age:

Expand your social sphere, befriend people different from you. Like we discussed earlier in the chapter, you never know what someone from a totally different background may have to share that you wouldn't know otherwise. This matters when you consider that it's not just what you know or who you know - it's who you know and who likes you that will determine your success. And nowhere is that more evident than the age divide in our peer groups. There's little to no push on young people to develop relationships with the number one group that can help you develop your future economic opportunity: adults. Try reaching out to older people like your extended family, your teachers, your supervisors, and coworkers who have several years' experience over you. They're brimming with knowledge and ready to share, so long as you ask.

Who are three people older than you by at least ten years you can reach out to today to build bridges in your life?

Name	Contact Info

Instead of holding people at arms' length, when you encounter someone very different from you in your program or job, get to know them! Approach them with an open and kind heart - and no matter what you do, don't ever go up to them and say, "You're X. Tell me about it."

Try asking them about other things: their hobbies, their free time, what brought them to the program, and what they're hoping to get out of it. By bridging cultural gaps, you're not just putting yourself in a position to challenge your own limiting stereotypes and find genuine friendships, but you're eliminating some barriers to social capital. Think about it:

if you're trapped in circles surrounded by your own demographic, it's inevitable that you'll encounter some repetitions in your potential for connections. By branching out and making new friends from all kinds of backgrounds and perspectives, you open yourself up to new levels of opportunity and new chances to foster a diverse social capital framework that can change your life.

One of the arenas that this respect comes in to play the most is with gender. Gender is an evolving topic in our world, and pronouns (the words "he," "she," or "they") matter. The best way to engage with coworkers who are trans* or gender non-conforming is by addressing them using the name and pronouns they ask you to use. If you aren't sure about the correct pronouns, ask them one-on-one (avoid big groups because that can put them in potentially life-threatening situations if someone in the group is homophobic or transphobic and violent). A great way to ask is simply, "Hey, X. What are your preferred pronouns? Mine are..." By sharing your own and asking them theirs, you are showing yourself to be a person they can rely on and trust as a coworker.

Our world's a global one, and chances are you already know and enjoy things that are from a different background than you came from. Whether it's food you love, a musician you listen to, or a country you've always been taken by, the world is richer when you experience and are open to the things that the rest of the world has on offer.

Imagine times when you haven't been open to someone who approached you because of their different culture. What are at least three things you might have lost because of your closed-mindedness?

_____

What can you gain down the road by getting to know people from other cultures next time the opportunity presents itself?

_____

_____

_____

When you approach the world with these compassionate and empathetic lenses on the situation, you will be met with bountiful and life-changing results.

Friends on the Job

Once you start adopting these attitudes of openness and acceptance, you may find that suddenly you're making friends with your coworkers, no matter what their perspective or background is - and that's great. Sharing a workplace is a healthy and natural cornerstone of many adult friendships, and coworkers who share your interests and motivation can be a pivotal part of helping you grow as a person in the world of work. That being said, it's critical to hold up your professional boundaries with everyone at work. As you get tighter with your coworkers, you may start to backslide on making sure you're as productive at work as you were when you started - and that's something your boss notices. Think about it. Do you want a potential employer to call your old boss for a reference, only to hear them say that you talk way too much on the job?

That's not to say ignore your coworkers or avoid making friends. Just be mindful of your productivity and keep your number one focus where it ought to be: your work. This is also important because you never know who's nearby. As you get to know your coworkers and talk with them more and more, stay mindful of the words that come out of your mouth - especially around customers. While it's tempting to get casual and let swearing or personal content filter into your day-to-day talks with coworkers, dishing about parties, romance, or life problems while customers are around isn't exactly setting you up to be employee of the month. Not only could what you're talking about sell a negative image of the company you work for, you could make customers uncomfortable, talk about things that are inappropriate around children, or get in trouble. Your boss is going to notice sooner or later if you and your coworker are just chilling in the corner or stocking shelves in slow motion to talk together longer.

It isn't just your boss who will notice your slow work and distraction, either. Think about it. Have you ever been a customer and the employees were just hanging around, talking to each other? It probably didn't make you feel welcome in the store or encouraged to come back. In the age of Yelp, Google, and Facebook, it's crucial that you give customers a positive experience. You never know who's going to check in at your workplace and write a stellar (or abysmal) review calling out your customer service skills - or lack thereof. When no customers are around and you're working hard, talking with your coworkers is a wonderful way to brighten up your workplace. There is a way to healthily befriend your coworkers without putting your job at risk. Just remember why you're there - to work - and don't let a conversation, no matter how gripping, steer you away from what you're supposed to be doing.

Setting boundaries is vital. Without doing this, you invite inappropriate relationships, unprofessional behavior, and habits that can jeopardize your potential to secure references, skills, and future opportunities from your boss. Think back on some irresponsible things you've seen people doing on the clock, either as a customer or as a coworker:

_____

_____

_____

_____

_____

What kinds of consequences can each of these acts have?

_____

_____

Bad service and a distracted employee doesn't invite customers to keep shopping and sends a message about how little you care. While it may seem more fun to spend time with your friends, text, or hang out, it doesn't help you out in the long run and can make your summer job nothing more than a waste of your time.

Boundaries, boundaries, boundaries. They can be diffi-cult to enforce, especially when you're just starting out as an employee. It can be hard to shut down a new friend to go wipe down tables instead, but it pays off in the long run, and your coworker will be motivated by your choices and get their job done too. Drawing the line is important, but it doesn't have to be ice cold, either. Try saying something like this, but in your own words, to get you and your coworker back on track: "I seriously love what we're talking about, but what if we picked it back up after work? I gotta go do X, Y, and Z right now."

When's a time your coworkers distracted you from your work?

_____

_____

If and when it comes up again, what could you say the next

time you need to rein in the distracted talk with your coworkers while still holding onto your positive friendships and relationships with them?

_____

_____

Of course, keeping on task gets even harder when friends who aren't your coworkers show up at your work-place. When you get a job, the friends you already have may want to come by and see what's up, score a free drink, share their latest escapades, or show you some YouTube videos. As tempting as it is to kick back when your bestie strolls in, it's with these friends who don't work with you that setting boundaries is more important than ever; if you're chilling with someone who isn't even an employee and you aren't doing work your boss is going to question what exactly you're getting paid for, and you could find yourself unemployed a few weeks earlier than planned that summer, without a reference for the next job, and no better off than you were before.

When was a time your friend showed up at your job?

_____

How did it feel?

_____

Were you more or less productive while your friend was there? How did you spend that time?

_____

_____

If you were an employer, how would you feel about the employee whose friends were always showing up?

_____

What about the employee who spent their time keeping things clean, interacting with customers, and asking what else can be done?

_____

Which of those two employees would you rather give a reference letter to? Why?

_____

_____

We're not here to suggest you should go ahead and give your friends the cold shoulder when they show up. Say "hi." Be happy to see them – but set boundaries for yourself. One simple and noninflammatory way to acknowledge your friend while letting them know you have to get moving is by saying something along the lines of, "I gotta get back to work, but I'll hit you up once I'm off the clock!" This lets them know that you need to get back to work and signals that you have tasks on your plate while showing you value their time and friendship. After all, your future economic opportunities are on the line, and if the friend you're hanging with is worth holding onto, they'll respect the boundaries you set and be happy to see you're putting your future first.

Which of your friends is most likely to come to your work-place and try to distract you?

_____

What can you say to them that will let them know you're busy?

_____

Remember: a good friendship is one that encourages you to be the best version of yourself possible and build up your FEO. If your friend is a keeper, they'll be down to support you on your path toward financial abundance and a future ripe with opportunities, connections, and experience.

Crushing on the Clock

Romance is a wonderful thing. When love is in the air, it can feel like the world is your oyster, and especially when you're younger, it can feel like love is around just about every other corner. But there's a time and a place to prioritize romance - and it isn't while you're on the clock. While you're working, you'll be spending a lot of time with your coworkers. You may even think they're cute. But above all other things - avoid romance with your coworkers. Flirting isn't on the table while you're at work. Not only will your boss notice your distraction, you may be making your coworker uncomfortable without realizing it. Maybe the person you're working with hasn't read this book and doesn't know the tips you have for setting boundaries. Maybe they're afraid that if they turn you down, you'll make it hard to work with them. Maybe they're afraid of starting drama by shutting the flirting down.

The best thing to do? Avoid putting your coworkers in a bad situation in the first place. Be polite; don't say anything to a coworker you wouldn't be comfortable saying in front of your mom (or your boss, for that matter). To steer clear of putting someone in a situation that makes working miserable, just don't comment on their appearance, positively or negatively, and never ask them on a date. Things like this make for a sour work environment that can land you in a world of trouble. Thanks to the #metoo movement, many people are finding their voices and standing up to situations that make them uncomfortable, and more bosses are feeling the pressure to keep hold their colleagues accountable. If you haven't done so before, search #metoo on Twitter or Instagram. Read up on the culture and be part of the solution.

These boundaries don't stop at your coworkers. When interacting with customers, there's an even bigger necessity for all interactions to be professional, not an opportunity to make new friends. Customers show up at your workplace to get their coffee or groceries, or to receive a service. They're not coming to the restaurant on the prowl for a love connection. Flirting with a customer can make them uncomfortable. When you flirt with a customer you risk them, at best, never coming back and your actions costing the company a customer. At worst, the customer can choose to report you to your boss, putting your job and FEO on the line.

Even if you're 99% sure the feeling is mutual, still greet the situation with professionalism and put your job first. If your gut is right and the other person feels the same way, then your drive and dedication to your job will only serve you. What's more impressive than being motivated to succeed?

Be Smart! Be safe!

Above all other things, make sure you're exercising safety as you head out into the working world, both with who you spend time with after work, and the job tasks themselves.

Nowadays, many protections are in place to help you stay safe on the job. If you're under eighteen, it can be frustrating to not be allowed to operate heavy machinery, baking, or deli equipment, but learning the other jobs in the field is a great first step to learning the ropes. You'll have the rest of your life to operate the equipment. For now, master the work you're allowed to, and you'll be more than equipped to learn how to use the machinery down the line.

More than that, be wary when you interact with people. Use your instincts. Adults often do have your best interests in mind, but there are people who will take advantage of you. If an adult sets off any alarm bells in your head, listen to them.

An adult, supervisor, coworker, or customer should never say something or ask you to do something that makes you feel unsafe. If something does happen, it's their fault, but take preventative steps when possible: don't go places with adults that you don't know and that aren't part of your program. Only spend time with the adults who run the program in approved settings and never meet them at their home or somewhere you'll be alone. And remember: if an adult is acting suspiciously, harassing you, or making you otherwise uncomfortable, remember that it is most likely not you misinterpreting a situation. Speak up, don't let adults walk all over you, and always put your safety first.

When you're communicating, connecting, and building up your FEO wisely, you'll be ready to make the most of your summer job experience.

Ch 8: When the Summer is Over

Using Summer Work Experience to Build Opportunity Connections

In the streets, we all know the importance of surrounding yourself with people who have your back. But what does that really mean? All too often, "having your back" translates to someone who will do dirt with you and help you ultimately lose your life, freedom, or future economic opportunity. What if having someone's back meant the opposite? What would it look like if the people who had you were there to support your life, freedom, and FEO-building?

In the workplace, you have the chance to make connections like that for your future. Those people are the ones with good reputations who are willing to vouch for you and give you a recommendation for a job down the line. Because when two equally qualified candidates reach for the same opportunity, it's always the one with the personal connection that lands that job. This is even more crucial when you find yourself up against applicants who are even more qualified than you. To get your first big break, you need to inundate the hiring manager with a number of credible people who are willing to vouch for your skills, motivation, and ability to thrive.

To get started, you have to know who in your life to trust, and who to bust. Sometimes, this can be easier said than done. We all have had a relationship or friendship that we're tangled up in, despite it bringing us down in real life.

What not everyone realizes is that there's always a way out of those entanglements, even if it seems impossible now. Just remember: your life, freedom, and future economic opportunity depend on those changes.

So how do you build those connections during your work experience to call upon down the line? First, avoid these key recommendation killers from day one:

1) Being consistently late
2) Having a stink face or salty attitude
3) Not completing your tasks
4) Texting on the job
5) Giving bad customer service
6) Never taking the time to learn or do more work

Beyond avoiding these six things, what you can do on the job to help show your supervisors and co-workers that you are a solid person to give a reference to?

1) _____
2) _____
3) _____
4) _____
5) _____

If you play your card right during your summer job program, you'll make a wealth of valuable connections and lay the groundwork with people who genuinely find you to be a trustworthy and dedicated worker. Remember – one thing that holds employees back from being great is their inability to both do the work and communicate future goals clearly. Solidify the connections you make now by being explicit! Ask to keep in touch and serve as references for one another down the road. Don't let opportunity to connect pass you by.

Make those connections before the program ends. Be the coworker you wish you had and ask the people you work with to be your references. While you work with co-workers and supervisors, share your goals and how you're working toward them, and be direct about what those goals are - especially when talking to your boss. The more people you can have in your corner asserting that you're a goal-mind-ed, focused employee, the better.

It can be overwhelming to think of reaching out to coworkers and supervisors, and our culture doesn't encourage us to think about the ways we have a lot to offer. But you do. Your work in your summer job program is proof of your own ability to thrive. What are three strengths you have as an employee that make you worthy of asking your coworkers for their endorsement?

_____

_____

_____

There'll come a time down the road where you will have to reach out to folks that you know either very little or not at all to support you in your FEO journey. It can be intimidating, but reaching out to create those bridges may yield results that surprise you. Don't be pushy, but do communicate your goals, your abilities, and why you're asking for their advice.

1)What is one thing you did last week to connect with someone?

_____

_____

2)   What is one thing you could have done to connect with someone, but chose not to?

_____

_____

3)   What could you do next time?

_____

_____

Don't let opportunity pass you by. Who is one summer supervisor you can approach for a reference letter?

_____

Ask them as soon as possible to be your reference down the line. When you ask them, remember that you are someone worth hiring...aren't you? Embody the attitude that you really are the best candidate for the job and practice writing a recommendation letter for yourself:

Dear _____,

   I am enthusiastic to recommend _____. I have known them for __ years.
   _____ has always displayed a high degree of _____ , _____, and _____. While working at _____ , they always _____ . In addition to their personal accomplishments as a _____ , they have proven their leadership abilities by _____ _____ _____. Moreover, they are a dependable team player – like the time _____ _____ _____. They have good _____, a mature _____, and are always eager to learn.
   It is my firm belief that _____ would be a remarkable asset to any organization, and I am happy to give them my recommendation.
   Sincerely,

[Your Signature]

[Your Name]

[Your Title]

While you can't exactly use this recommendation while applying for a job, keep the things you wrote down here in your mind when you ask your supervisors and coworkers for references. You are a valuable employee and have used your time in the program wisely to make the most of your opportunity. Keep your chin up, your shoulders back, and stay confident that you're making the right choices to build your FEO - because as long as you have done the things this book recommended, you've been slaying it.

Documenting Your FEO Journey

As your summer job draws to a close, everything you've learned and accomplished is fresh in your mind. But as summer creeps into fall, the things you did and how they influenced your life can start to fade. Don't let all you've done get lost as you get caught up in the present moment! By documenting the progress you've made on your FEO journey, you are keeping the foundations of an active resume that you can adapt and use for future job opportunities down the line.

You've started to build your FEO, and you've learned some great lessons along the way. What's the most important thing you've learned about success?

_____

_____

_____

What is your number one plan down the line regarding future income?

_____

_____

Money matters. The best way to keep making money is to land your next job, one that builds on the skills,   experiences, and references you spent so long cultivating this summer. And while you've definitely heard of a resume, take i t one step further and create an FEO resume. Your FEO resume is an updated snapshot of your FEO-journey-in-progress. With it, you can document the skills, experience, degrees, social capital connections, and credentials you spent the summer honing while you worked at your summer job.

So think back on everything from this summer: what experiences did you have? What talents did you uncover, or knowledge you internalize? You have already made a vast web of connections that saw your development first hand. By writing this all down, you'll be ready to pursue further work and educational opportunities down the line.

Your FEO Resume

_____

(First and Last Name)

_____

(Street Address)

_____

(City, State, Zip Code)

_____

(Telephone #)

Objective

(Be specific and identify the job you're applying for and the ultimate career you want as it relates to the position you're applying for. Be specific in what you say your objective is!)

Skills

☐ _____

☐ _____

☐ _____

(What skills do you know? Include things that are relevant, like Microsoft Word, as well as soft skills like customer service.)

Credentials

☐ _____

☐ _____

☐ _____

(What certifications of completion do you have?)

Experience

___/ ___/ _____

(Start Date [month/year] to End Date [month/year]), (Job Title), (Company Name)

_____

(Company Street Address)

_____

(City, State, Zip code)

☐ _____

☐ _____

☐ _____

(Job Duties – be specific!)

___/ ___/ _____

(Start Date [month/year] to End Date [month/year]), (Job Title), (Company Name)

_____

(Company Street Address)

_____

(City, State, Zip code)

☐_____

☐_____

☐_____

(Job Duties - be specific!)

Degrees

_____

(High School Name)

_____

(Graduation Date [month/year])

_____

(Street Address)

_____

(City, State, Zip code)

Networks

| _____ | _____ | _____ |
| (Name) | (Contact Info) | (Relationship) |

| _____ | _____ | _____ |
| (Name) | (Contact Info) | (Relationship) |

| _____ | _____ | _____ |
| (Name) | (Contact Info) | (Relationship) |

With the FEO Resume you have above, you're sure to be able to fill out any application down the line so well that the employers will look twice. Get ready: job number two is going to be worlds easier to land than the first ones.

What are some ways that knowing the ins and outs of your FEO Resume help your career?

_____

Take the resume you built above and make a real resume on a word document. But before you go in there scratching your head at how to format it – don't worry. There are hundreds of free on-line templates for building the best resume. If you're using Microsoft Word, click "File," then "New," and from there, you can type in "Resume" and will be taken to various templates to reflect your personal skillset and aesthetic. With this polished resume in hand, who knows what you can do?

The Credibility You Need

Although the summer job may be over, your social capital is not. So how do you continue to build social capital with your summer work supervisor and others? You must stay connected! While most people know that follow-up is important, few are masterful at it. Leaving one or two voicemails or sending a couple of e-mails is not follow-up. Your future career success will likely have more to do more with who you know, and who likes you, than what you know. Forgetting to stay in contact with those who helped you is economic suicide. Staying in contact with your summer work supervisor is not about nagging or harassing. It's about reminding. Remind them of the wonderful, valuable ways that they contributed to your growth and development and showing them the outcomes of their efforts.

Staying connected is acknowledgment, and people like to be acknowledged. Successful young people know that recognizing others makes them more receptive and willing to help. Really smart young people know that staying connected is much easier than trying to reconnect. You will need their help again. Don't lose the connection.

Here's how to do it - stay credible and communicate your credibility.

What do you think credibility means? We like to define credibility as the believability of a source or message. Basically, credibility is the summer job supervisor's assessment of your believability. To put it simply, they will do things for you if they believe in you. It's your job to make them believe.

There is a credibility problem in the United States, and we don't want you to be a part of it. In today's world of instant communication and lightning speed decision-making, establishing your credibility is becoming more challenging. Many internet celebrities are now more credible with the public than major news outlets. So, what can you do about your credibility? Use every accomplishment you make as an opportunity to establish and build your credibility. Take advantage of every one of those achievements, no matter how small, by communicating them to your former summer work supervisor. At DeJesus Solutions, we know that the best way to establish credibility is to demonstrate your commitment to your FEO. We call these FEO commitments.

You will build credibility with every adult by showcasing your accomplishments. There is no stronger builder of credibility – ever. To do this, you should focus on:

• Telling—Make adults believe and trust what you say. Tell them what active steps you took in since leaving the summer job program to build your FEO. This gives your message credibility, plus people always like to hear what steps young people are taking to improve their lives.

• Showing—Back up your statements with compelling evidence. Give your former summer work supervisor convincing evidence that you are making progress in your FEO (certificates, degrees, enrollment letters, photographs, videos, etc.). For example, if you want to convince a former supervisor that you have been pursuing your education, send them a copy of your most recent progress report. If you have been looking for work, mention the places where you have applied for a job.

• Calling—Call on others to back up your claims. You would be surprised by the power of a 2nd party. Similar to the reference letter activity above, having someone back up your claims is a powerful tool to establish credibility. It's simple to ask a teacher or community leader to write a blurb about your character and/or performance. Plus, you will be building more social capital along the way.

• Admitting—Be honest about your setbacks and be prepared to show your former summer work supervisor and others how you corrected yourself. People trust people who admit mistakes. Everyone makes them. When people don't admit mistakes, people know they are not telling the truth.

Writing letters, sending emails, scheduled visits, and phone calls are some of the many ways that you can and should stay connected to your summer work supervisor. At DeJesus Solutions, we know if you stay in contact with someone at least twice per year, you will forever be connected to that person and the opportunities they bring.

Conclusion

Signing up for a summer job or summer job program is a revolutionary step to improving the quality of your life now and for decades to come. You have taken control of your own life and are well on the road to making the most of your future. And now that you've started the journey, don't stop. Keep that momentum going. Join clubs in school that teach you valuable skills. Volunteer. Pour yourself into your education and recognize there's a way out and up into the life that you deserve: one that is financially abundant, safe, and full of meaningful connections and activities.

To keep that energy and drive going, join the MAKiN' iT Nation on-line at www.edwarddejesus.com. There you can connect with a web of likeminded young people eager to make the most of their lives and promote their life, freedom, and future economic opportunity.

#makinitnation #dejesusspeaks

Remember that it is not about talent. It's about hard work. Hard work always beats talent especially when talent doesn't want to work hard. We are a force. Together, we're unstoppable. You've come this far, and you'll go further.

I promise!

1: https://scholars.org/brief/how-summer-job-pro-grams-can-improve-young-people-and-disadvantaged-communities

2: https://www.scholastic.com/teachers/articles/teach-ing-content/history-child-labor/

3: https://www.investopedia.com/financial-edge/0610/top-5-benefits-of-a-summer-job---besides-pay.aspx

4: http://www.right.com/wps/wcm/connect/right-us-en/home/thoughtwire/categories/talent-work/networking-not-internet-cruising-still-lands-most-jobs-for-those-in-career-transition).

5: Dunbar, R. I. M. (1992). "Neocortex size as a constraint on group size in primates". Journal of Human Evolution. 22 (6): 469–493. doi:10.1016/0047-2484(92)90081-J.

About the Author

Edward DeJesus

Street Credible, Research-Backed and Impact Driven

More than 100,000 educators, policy-makers, and young adults unanimously agree that DeJesus' message about the importance of life, freedom and future economic opportunity is an important message that all young people need to hear.

Born and raised in the Bronx, NY, DeJesus is a top speaker at over 20 major youth conferences each year. As a former VIBE magazine editor puts it: "DeJesus' message hits home with the weight of a project building falling on your head. And once every brick has touched down, audiences will have a clear idea of what must be done."

Thirty years of experience in the trenches in some of the toughest neighborhoods and policy-making environments has prepared DeJesus to reveal the true social, political and cultural dynamics that keep so many youth from educational and workforce success. Through creative and inspirational storytelling mixed with cold hard facts, DeJesus argues that every community has the seeds to set up the structures that make a difference in their youth's future. And, through his message, audiences learn how to make these seeds grow.

Edward DeJesus is the President of DeJesus Solutions. Their mission is "No More Disconnected Youth." In the U.S. today, 4.6 million youth are disconnected from work and school, and millions more are struggling to hold on. DeJesus and his team create policy and programmatic solutions to build future economic opportunities for the most marginalized youth and young adults.

DeJesus is a W.K. Kellogg Foundation National Fellow and holds a Masters of Science in Management and Urban Policy Analysis from the New School for Social Research. He is the host of the MAKiN' iT Podcast and video learning series. His best selling book, MAKiN' iT is in use by hundreds of programs across the U.S. His work has been featured on NPR, in the Washington Post, the Baltimore Sun and the Miami Herald.

DeJesus has blended his love for reaching youth with an extraordinary ability to impact policy by conducting research on effective programs that help youth acquire and maintain jobs. DeJesus served as a youth policy expert for the Sar Levitan Center for Youth Policy at John Hopkins University and served on the Task Force on Employment Opportunities for young offenders for the U.S. Office of Juvenile Justice and Delinquency Prevention. He has served as a consultant to the Annie E. Casey Foundation, Charles Stewart Mott Foundation, the U.S. Dept. of Labor, and the National Education Association.

In his spare time, DeJesus competes in Ironman triathlons.

NOTES

NOTES

NOTES

NOTES

NOTES

NOTES

ORDER FORM

Name:_____

Organization: _____

Address:

_____

City: _____State:_____ Zip:_____

Phone: _____ e-mail:_____

Credit Card #: Visa/MC/Amex:_____

Exp Date: _____ CVV#_____

Please make **Check** payable to:
DeJesus Solutions
6925 Oakland Mills Rd #355
Columbia, MD 21045
301-323-8780
Or email form to
office@dejesusspeaks.com

www.edwarddejesus.com

Item	Quantity	Conf price*/Regular	Total
Summer Job Success		$12.95 100 or more: $9.95 each	
MAKiN' iT		$15.95	
Making Connections Work		$14.95	
MAKiN' iT CURRICULUM, Poster set and Scale		$750.00	
		Sub total	
		Shipping/Handling 3% of total order or 6.99 whichever is greater	
		TOTAL	

56338953R00061

Made in the USA
Columbia, SC
23 April 2019